Watercolor Garden Password Logbook

Artwork by: Pobytov

THIS BOOK BELONGS TO

_____

A

WEBSITE	
USERNAME	
PASSWORD	
NOTES	

WEBSITE	
USERNAME	
PASSWORD	
NOTES	

WEBSITE	
USERNAME	
PASSWORD	
NOTES	

A

WEBSITE	
USERNAME	
PASSWORD	
NOTES	

WEBSITE	
USERNAME	
PASSWORD	
NOTES	

WEBSITE	
USERNAME	
PASSWORD	
NOTES	

A

WEBSITE	
USERNAME	
PASSWORD	
NOTES	

WEBSITE	
USERNAME	
PASSWORD	
NOTES	

WEBSITE	
USERNAME	
PASSWORD	
NOTES	

WEBSITE	
USERNAME	
PASSWORD	
NOTES	

WEBSITE	
USERNAME	
PASSWORD	
NOTES	

WEBSITE	
USERNAME	
PASSWORD	
NOTES	

B

WEBSITE	
USERNAME	
PASSWORD	
NOTES	

WEBSITE	
USERNAME	
PASSWORD	
NOTES	

WEBSITE	
USERNAME	
PASSWORD	
NOTES	

WEBSITE	
USERNAME	
PASSWORD	
NOTES	

WEBSITE	
USERNAME	
PASSWORD	
NOTES	

WEBSITE	
USERNAME	
PASSWORD	
NOTES	

B

WEBSITE	
USERNAME	
PASSWORD	
NOTES	

WEBSITE	
USERNAME	
PASSWORD	
NOTES	

WEBSITE	
USERNAME	
PASSWORD	
NOTES	

B

WEBSITE	
USERNAME	
PASSWORD	
NOTES	

WEBSITE	
USERNAME	
PASSWORD	
NOTES	

WEBSITE	
USERNAME	
PASSWORD	
NOTES	

C

WEBSITE	
USERNAME	
PASSWORD	
NOTES	

WEBSITE	
USERNAME	
PASSWORD	
NOTES	

WEBSITE	
USERNAME	
PASSWORD	
NOTES	

C

WEBSITE	
USERNAME	
PASSWORD	
NOTES	

WEBSITE	
USERNAME	
PASSWORD	
NOTES	

WEBSITE	
USERNAME	
PASSWORD	
NOTES	

C

WEBSITE	
USERNAME	
PASSWORD	
NOTES	

WEBSITE	
USERNAME	
PASSWORD	
NOTES	

WEBSITE	
USERNAME	
PASSWORD	
NOTES	

WEBSITE	
USERNAME	
PASSWORD	
NOTES	

WEBSITE	
USERNAME	
PASSWORD	
NOTES	

WEBSITE	
USERNAME	
PASSWORD	
NOTES	

D

WEBSITE	
USERNAME	
PASSWORD	
NOTES	

WEBSITE	
USERNAME	
PASSWORD	
NOTES	

WEBSITE	
USERNAME	
PASSWORD	
NOTES	

WEBSITE	
USERNAME	
PASSWORD	
NOTES	

WEBSITE	
USERNAME	
PASSWORD	
NOTES	

WEBSITE	
USERNAME	
PASSWORD	
NOTES	

D

WEBSITE	
USERNAME	
PASSWORD	
NOTES	

WEBSITE	
USERNAME	
PASSWORD	
NOTES	

WEBSITE	
USERNAME	
PASSWORD	
NOTES	

D

WEBSITE	
USERNAME	
PASSWORD	
NOTES	

WEBSITE	
USERNAME	
PASSWORD	
NOTES	

WEBSITE	
USERNAME	
PASSWORD	
NOTES	

E

WEBSITE	
USERNAME	
PASSWORD	
NOTES	

WEBSITE	
USERNAME	
PASSWORD	
NOTES	

WEBSITE	
USERNAME	
PASSWORD	
NOTES	

E

WEBSITE	
USERNAME	
PASSWORD	
NOTES	

WEBSITE	
USERNAME	
PASSWORD	
NOTES	

WEBSITE	
USERNAME	
PASSWORD	
NOTES	

E

WEBSITE	
USERNAME	
PASSWORD	
NOTES	

WEBSITE	
USERNAME	
PASSWORD	
NOTES	

WEBSITE	
USERNAME	
PASSWORD	
NOTES	

E

WEBSITE	
USERNAME	
PASSWORD	
NOTES	

WEBSITE	
USERNAME	
PASSWORD	
NOTES	

WEBSITE	
USERNAME	
PASSWORD	
NOTES	

F

WEBSITE	
USERNAME	
PASSWORD	
NOTES	

WEBSITE	
USERNAME	
PASSWORD	
NOTES	

WEBSITE	
USERNAME	
PASSWORD	
NOTES	

F

WEBSITE	
USERNAME	
PASSWORD	
NOTES	

WEBSITE	
USERNAME	
PASSWORD	
NOTES	

WEBSITE	
USERNAME	
PASSWORD	
NOTES	

F

WEBSITE	
USERNAME	
PASSWORD	
NOTES	

WEBSITE	
USERNAME	
PASSWORD	
NOTES	

WEBSITE	
USERNAME	
PASSWORD	
NOTES	

F

WEBSITE	
USERNAME	
PASSWORD	
NOTES	

WEBSITE	
USERNAME	
PASSWORD	
NOTES	

WEBSITE	
USERNAME	
PASSWORD	
NOTES	

G

WEBSITE	
USERNAME	
PASSWORD	
NOTES	

WEBSITE	
USERNAME	
PASSWORD	
NOTES	

WEBSITE	
USERNAME	
PASSWORD	
NOTES	

G

WEBSITE	
USERNAME	
PASSWORD	
NOTES	

WEBSITE	
USERNAME	
PASSWORD	
NOTES	

WEBSITE	
USERNAME	
PASSWORD	
NOTES	

G

WEBSITE	
USERNAME	
PASSWORD	
NOTES	

WEBSITE	
USERNAME	
PASSWORD	
NOTES	

WEBSITE	
USERNAME	
PASSWORD	
NOTES	

G

WEBSITE	
USERNAME	
PASSWORD	
NOTES	

WEBSITE	
USERNAME	
PASSWORD	
NOTES	

WEBSITE	
USERNAME	
PASSWORD	
NOTES	

H

WEBSITE	
USERNAME	
PASSWORD	
NOTES	

WEBSITE	
USERNAME	
PASSWORD	
NOTES	

WEBSITE	
USERNAME	
PASSWORD	
NOTES	

H

WEBSITE	
USERNAME	
PASSWORD	
NOTES	

WEBSITE	
USERNAME	
PASSWORD	
NOTES	

WEBSITE	
USERNAME	
PASSWORD	
NOTES	

H

WEBSITE	
USERNAME	
PASSWORD	
NOTES	

WEBSITE	
USERNAME	
PASSWORD	
NOTES	

WEBSITE	
USERNAME	
PASSWORD	
NOTES	

H

WEBSITE	
USERNAME	
PASSWORD	
NOTES	

WEBSITE	
USERNAME	
PASSWORD	
NOTES	

WEBSITE	
USERNAME	
PASSWORD	
NOTES	

I

WEBSITE	
USERNAME	
PASSWORD	
NOTES	

WEBSITE	
USERNAME	
PASSWORD	
NOTES	

WEBSITE	
USERNAME	
PASSWORD	
NOTES	

I

WEBSITE	
USERNAME	
PASSWORD	
NOTES	

WEBSITE	
USERNAME	
PASSWORD	
NOTES	

WEBSITE	
USERNAME	
PASSWORD	
NOTES	

I

WEBSITE	
USERNAME	
PASSWORD	
NOTES	

WEBSITE	
USERNAME	
PASSWORD	
NOTES	

WEBSITE	
USERNAME	
PASSWORD	
NOTES	

WEBSITE	
USERNAME	
PASSWORD	
NOTES	

WEBSITE	
USERNAME	
PASSWORD	
NOTES	

WEBSITE	
USERNAME	
PASSWORD	
NOTES	

J

WEBSITE	
USERNAME	
PASSWORD	
NOTES	

WEBSITE	
USERNAME	
PASSWORD	
NOTES	

WEBSITE	
USERNAME	
PASSWORD	
NOTES	

J

WEBSITE	
USERNAME	
PASSWORD	
NOTES	

WEBSITE	
USERNAME	
PASSWORD	
NOTES	

WEBSITE	
USERNAME	
PASSWORD	
NOTES	

J

WEBSITE	
USERNAME	
PASSWORD	
NOTES	

WEBSITE	
USERNAME	
PASSWORD	
NOTES	

WEBSITE	
USERNAME	
PASSWORD	
NOTES	

J

WEBSITE	
USERNAME	
PASSWORD	
NOTES	

WEBSITE	
USERNAME	
PASSWORD	
NOTES	

WEBSITE	
USERNAME	
PASSWORD	
NOTES	

K

WEBSITE	
USERNAME	
PASSWORD	
NOTES	

WEBSITE	
USERNAME	
PASSWORD	
NOTES	

WEBSITE	
USERNAME	
PASSWORD	
NOTES	

K

WEBSITE	
USERNAME	
PASSWORD	
NOTES	

WEBSITE	
USERNAME	
PASSWORD	
NOTES	

WEBSITE	
USERNAME	
PASSWORD	
NOTES	

K

WEBSITE	
USERNAME	
PASSWORD	
NOTES	

WEBSITE	
USERNAME	
PASSWORD	
NOTES	

WEBSITE	
USERNAME	
PASSWORD	
NOTES	

K

WEBSITE	
USERNAME	
PASSWORD	
NOTES	

WEBSITE	
USERNAME	
PASSWORD	
NOTES	

WEBSITE	
USERNAME	
PASSWORD	
NOTES	

L

WEBSITE	
USERNAME	
PASSWORD	
NOTES	

WEBSITE	
USERNAME	
PASSWORD	
NOTES	

WEBSITE	
USERNAME	
PASSWORD	
NOTES	

L

WEBSITE	
USERNAME	
PASSWORD	
NOTES	

WEBSITE	
USERNAME	
PASSWORD	
NOTES	

WEBSITE	
USERNAME	
PASSWORD	
NOTES	

L

WEBSITE	
USERNAME	
PASSWORD	
NOTES	

WEBSITE	
USERNAME	
PASSWORD	
NOTES	

WEBSITE	
USERNAME	
PASSWORD	
NOTES	

L

WEBSITE	
USERNAME	
PASSWORD	
NOTES	

WEBSITE	
USERNAME	
PASSWORD	
NOTES	

WEBSITE	
USERNAME	
PASSWORD	
NOTES	

M

WEBSITE	
USERNAME	
PASSWORD	
NOTES	

WEBSITE	
USERNAME	
PASSWORD	
NOTES	

WEBSITE	
USERNAME	
PASSWORD	
NOTES	

M

WEBSITE	
USERNAME	
PASSWORD	
NOTES	

WEBSITE	
USERNAME	
PASSWORD	
NOTES	

WEBSITE	
USERNAME	
PASSWORD	
NOTES	

M

WEBSITE	
USERNAME	
PASSWORD	
NOTES	

WEBSITE	
USERNAME	
PASSWORD	
NOTES	

WEBSITE	
USERNAME	
PASSWORD	
NOTES	

M

WEBSITE	
USERNAME	
PASSWORD	
NOTES	

WEBSITE	
USERNAME	
PASSWORD	
NOTES	

WEBSITE	
USERNAME	
PASSWORD	
NOTES	

N

WEBSITE	
USERNAME	
PASSWORD	
NOTES	

WEBSITE	
USERNAME	
PASSWORD	
NOTES	

WEBSITE	
USERNAME	
PASSWORD	
NOTES	

WEBSITE	
USERNAME	
PASSWORD	
NOTES	

WEBSITE	
USERNAME	
PASSWORD	
NOTES	

WEBSITE	
USERNAME	
PASSWORD	
NOTES	

N

WEBSITE	
USERNAME	
PASSWORD	
NOTES	

WEBSITE	
USERNAME	
PASSWORD	
NOTES	

WEBSITE	
USERNAME	
PASSWORD	
NOTES	

N

WEBSITE	
USERNAME	
PASSWORD	
NOTES	

WEBSITE	
USERNAME	
PASSWORD	
NOTES	

WEBSITE	
USERNAME	
PASSWORD	
NOTES	

O

WEBSITE	
USERNAME	
PASSWORD	
NOTES	

WEBSITE	
USERNAME	
PASSWORD	
NOTES	

WEBSITE	
USERNAME	
PASSWORD	
NOTES	

O

WEBSITE	
USERNAME	
PASSWORD	
NOTES	

WEBSITE	
USERNAME	
PASSWORD	
NOTES	

WEBSITE	
USERNAME	
PASSWORD	
NOTES	

O

WEBSITE	
USERNAME	
PASSWORD	
NOTES	

WEBSITE	
USERNAME	
PASSWORD	
NOTES	

WEBSITE	
USERNAME	
PASSWORD	
NOTES	

O

WEBSITE	
USERNAME	
PASSWORD	
NOTES	

WEBSITE	
USERNAME	
PASSWORD	
NOTES	

WEBSITE	
USERNAME	
PASSWORD	
NOTES	

P

WEBSITE	
USERNAME	
PASSWORD	
NOTES	

WEBSITE	
USERNAME	
PASSWORD	
NOTES	

WEBSITE	
USERNAME	
PASSWORD	
NOTES	

WEBSITE	
USERNAME	
PASSWORD	
NOTES	

WEBSITE	
USERNAME	
PASSWORD	
NOTES	

WEBSITE	
USERNAME	
PASSWORD	
NOTES	

P

WEBSITE	
USERNAME	
PASSWORD	
NOTES	

WEBSITE	
USERNAME	
PASSWORD	
NOTES	

WEBSITE	
USERNAME	
PASSWORD	
NOTES	

P

WEBSITE	
USERNAME	
PASSWORD	
NOTES	

WEBSITE	
USERNAME	
PASSWORD	
NOTES	

WEBSITE	
USERNAME	
PASSWORD	
NOTES	

Q

WEBSITE	
USERNAME	
PASSWORD	
NOTES	

WEBSITE	
USERNAME	
PASSWORD	
NOTES	

WEBSITE	
USERNAME	
PASSWORD	
NOTES	

Q

WEBSITE	
USERNAME	
PASSWORD	
NOTES	

WEBSITE	
USERNAME	
PASSWORD	
NOTES	

WEBSITE	
USERNAME	
PASSWORD	
NOTES	

Q

WEBSITE	
USERNAME	
PASSWORD	
NOTES	

WEBSITE	
USERNAME	
PASSWORD	
NOTES	

WEBSITE	
USERNAME	
PASSWORD	
NOTES	

Q

WEBSITE	
USERNAME	
PASSWORD	
NOTES	

WEBSITE	
USERNAME	
PASSWORD	
NOTES	

WEBSITE	
USERNAME	
PASSWORD	
NOTES	

R

WEBSITE	
USERNAME	
PASSWORD	
NOTES	

WEBSITE	
USERNAME	
PASSWORD	
NOTES	

WEBSITE	
USERNAME	
PASSWORD	
NOTES	

R

WEBSITE	
USERNAME	
PASSWORD	
NOTES	

WEBSITE	
USERNAME	
PASSWORD	
NOTES	

WEBSITE	
USERNAME	
PASSWORD	
NOTES	

R

WEBSITE	
USERNAME	
PASSWORD	
NOTES	

WEBSITE	
USERNAME	
PASSWORD	
NOTES	

WEBSITE	
USERNAME	
PASSWORD	
NOTES	

WEBSITE	
USERNAME	
PASSWORD	
NOTES	

WEBSITE	
USERNAME	
PASSWORD	
NOTES	

WEBSITE	
USERNAME	
PASSWORD	
NOTES	

S

WEBSITE	
USERNAME	
PASSWORD	
NOTES	

WEBSITE	
USERNAME	
PASSWORD	
NOTES	

WEBSITE	
USERNAME	
PASSWORD	
NOTES	

S

WEBSITE	
USERNAME	
PASSWORD	
NOTES	

WEBSITE	
USERNAME	
PASSWORD	
NOTES	

WEBSITE	
USERNAME	
PASSWORD	
NOTES	

S

WEBSITE	
USERNAME	
PASSWORD	
NOTES	

WEBSITE	
USERNAME	
PASSWORD	
NOTES	

WEBSITE	
USERNAME	
PASSWORD	
NOTES	

S

WEBSITE	
USERNAME	
PASSWORD	
NOTES	

WEBSITE	
USERNAME	
PASSWORD	
NOTES	

WEBSITE	
USERNAME	
PASSWORD	
NOTES	

T

WEBSITE	
USERNAME	
PASSWORD	
NOTES	

WEBSITE	
USERNAME	
PASSWORD	
NOTES	

WEBSITE	
USERNAME	
PASSWORD	
NOTES	

WEBSITE	
USERNAME	
PASSWORD	
NOTES	

WEBSITE	
USERNAME	
PASSWORD	
NOTES	

WEBSITE	
USERNAME	
PASSWORD	
NOTES	

T

WEBSITE	
USERNAME	
PASSWORD	
NOTES	

WEBSITE	
USERNAME	
PASSWORD	
NOTES	

WEBSITE	
USERNAME	
PASSWORD	
NOTES	

T

WEBSITE	
USERNAME	
PASSWORD	
NOTES	

WEBSITE	
USERNAME	
PASSWORD	
NOTES	

WEBSITE	
USERNAME	
PASSWORD	
NOTES	

U

WEBSITE	
USERNAME	
PASSWORD	
NOTES	

WEBSITE	
USERNAME	
PASSWORD	
NOTES	

WEBSITE	
USERNAME	
PASSWORD	
NOTES	

U

WEBSITE	
USERNAME	
PASSWORD	
NOTES	

WEBSITE	
USERNAME	
PASSWORD	
NOTES	

WEBSITE	
USERNAME	
PASSWORD	
NOTES	

U

WEBSITE	
USERNAME	
PASSWORD	
NOTES	

WEBSITE	
USERNAME	
PASSWORD	
NOTES	

WEBSITE	
USERNAME	
PASSWORD	
NOTES	

U

WEBSITE	
USERNAME	
PASSWORD	
NOTES	

WEBSITE	
USERNAME	
PASSWORD	
NOTES	

WEBSITE	
USERNAME	
PASSWORD	
NOTES	

V

WEBSITE	
USERNAME	
PASSWORD	
NOTES	

WEBSITE	
USERNAME	
PASSWORD	
NOTES	

WEBSITE	
USERNAME	
PASSWORD	
NOTES	

V

WEBSITE	
USERNAME	
PASSWORD	
NOTES	

WEBSITE	
USERNAME	
PASSWORD	
NOTES	

WEBSITE	
USERNAME	
PASSWORD	
NOTES	

V

WEBSITE	
USERNAME	
PASSWORD	
NOTES	

WEBSITE	
USERNAME	
PASSWORD	
NOTES	

WEBSITE	
USERNAME	
PASSWORD	
NOTES	

V

WEBSITE	
USERNAME	
PASSWORD	
NOTES	

WEBSITE	
USERNAME	
PASSWORD	
NOTES	

WEBSITE	
USERNAME	
PASSWORD	
NOTES	

W

WEBSITE	
USERNAME	
PASSWORD	
NOTES	

WEBSITE	
USERNAME	
PASSWORD	
NOTES	

WEBSITE	
USERNAME	
PASSWORD	
NOTES	

W

WEBSITE	
USERNAME	
PASSWORD	
NOTES	

WEBSITE	
USERNAME	
PASSWORD	
NOTES	

WEBSITE	
USERNAME	
PASSWORD	
NOTES	

W

WEBSITE	
USERNAME	
PASSWORD	
NOTES	

WEBSITE	
USERNAME	
PASSWORD	
NOTES	

WEBSITE	
USERNAME	
PASSWORD	
NOTES	

W

WEBSITE	
USERNAME	
PASSWORD	
NOTES	

WEBSITE	
USERNAME	
PASSWORD	
NOTES	

WEBSITE	
USERNAME	
PASSWORD	
NOTES	

X

WEBSITE	
USERNAME	
PASSWORD	
NOTES	

WEBSITE	
USERNAME	
PASSWORD	
NOTES	

WEBSITE	
USERNAME	
PASSWORD	
NOTES	

X

WEBSITE	
USERNAME	
PASSWORD	
NOTES	

WEBSITE	
USERNAME	
PASSWORD	
NOTES	

WEBSITE	
USERNAME	
PASSWORD	
NOTES	

X

WEBSITE	
USERNAME	
PASSWORD	
NOTES	

WEBSITE	
USERNAME	
PASSWORD	
NOTES	

WEBSITE	
USERNAME	
PASSWORD	
NOTES	

X

WEBSITE	
USERNAME	
PASSWORD	
NOTES	

WEBSITE	
USERNAME	
PASSWORD	
NOTES	

WEBSITE	
USERNAME	
PASSWORD	
NOTES	

Y

WEBSITE	
USERNAME	
PASSWORD	
NOTES	

WEBSITE	
USERNAME	
PASSWORD	
NOTES	

WEBSITE	
USERNAME	
PASSWORD	
NOTES	

WEBSITE	
USERNAME	
PASSWORD	
NOTES	

WEBSITE	
USERNAME	
PASSWORD	
NOTES	

WEBSITE	
USERNAME	
PASSWORD	
NOTES	

Y

WEBSITE	
USERNAME	
PASSWORD	
NOTES	

WEBSITE	
USERNAME	
PASSWORD	
NOTES	

WEBSITE	
USERNAME	
PASSWORD	
NOTES	

Y

WEBSITE	
USERNAME	
PASSWORD	
NOTES	

WEBSITE	
USERNAME	
PASSWORD	
NOTES	

WEBSITE	
USERNAME	
PASSWORD	
NOTES	

Z

WEBSITE	
USERNAME	
PASSWORD	
NOTES	

WEBSITE	
USERNAME	
PASSWORD	
NOTES	

WEBSITE	
USERNAME	
PASSWORD	
NOTES	

Z

WEBSITE	
USERNAME	
PASSWORD	
NOTES	

WEBSITE	
USERNAME	
PASSWORD	
NOTES	

WEBSITE	
USERNAME	
PASSWORD	
NOTES	

Z

WEBSITE	
USERNAME	
PASSWORD	
NOTES	

WEBSITE	
USERNAME	
PASSWORD	
NOTES	

WEBSITE	
USERNAME	
PASSWORD	
NOTES	

WEBSITE	
USERNAME	
PASSWORD	
NOTES	

WEBSITE	
USERNAME	
PASSWORD	
NOTES	

WEBSITE	
USERNAME	
PASSWORD	
NOTES